# The Book of
# Nicknames

### Some Are Simple and Some
### Unusual but They Are All Unique

## Rodney D. Brooks

authorHOUSE®

AuthorHouse™
1663 Liberty Drive
Bloomington, IN 47403
www.authorhouse.com
Phone: 1 (800) 839-8640

Published by AuthorHouse    06/13/2016

ISBN: 978-1-5246-1124-8 (sc)
ISBN: 978-1-5246-1123-1 (e)

Library of Congress Control Number: 2016908830

Print information available on the last page.

# Contents

# Acknowledgements

To say this fun adventure of putting together this information was all done by me alone would be far from the truth. From family member to friends; these sources gave me data and inspiration to compile our list.

To my family members: Nancy Brooks, Rhonda Brooks, Breanne Brooks, Ben Brooks and Rodney Brooks Jr., thank you for putting up with me these last several months of constantly nagging you about some of your friends and acquaintances interesting nicknames that were not to inappropriate (what I am really saying is to vulgar). To my co-workers who jumped right on it when I asked each of you to give me a list of some of the nicknames that you have come across in your families and through your acquaintances. Thank you Sinnessa Wilburn, Robert Bohannon, and Deena Crane. I really appreciate your fun attitude about doing it. A special thanks to my friend Tracy Rule, who has always come through for me whenever I ask her for any type of information. So in case someone wants to know who is Tooter, just ask Tracy.

Although this was some time very taxing on me I thoroughly enjoyed it over the past six plus months. One thing that I did find very interesting in my quest of putting this data together; you may think that only one person may have such a unique nickname only to find out several other people may have that same nickname and they could be of a different race or gender.

Special thanks to God and my Lord and Savior Jesus Christ who has given me the ability to try and put things together with in an effort to support those who are homeless, stranded and down and out.

# Introduction

What comes to your mind when you think of a nickname. Does a specific individual come to mind or do you think about your own nickname if you have one. Driving home one day and reminiscing on the past (that happens when you hit 50 I am told) I started to laugh as I thought about this nickname that my uncles and had given a gentlemen who would come and visit their neighbor next door in the duplex where they lived. It was a very unusual nickname but the majority of nicknames are usually unusual.

Nicknames can be used to describe the character of an individual, the look of an individual, or a quick way of shortening the person's name.

Some nicknames are given by others to individual while some nicknames are derived by the individual. I have compiled a list of nicknames that I have come across in my life time as well as nicknames that some of my colleagues, friends and family members have sent me. I have tried to stay away from those that can be deemed offensive or that are long as a compound sentence. I have also dropped the "The" in front of some nicknames for example "The Comforter" or "The Inventor" as an example. Some nicknames can sometimes only be understood by certain cultures, families or regions The unique things about nicknames is that it does not matter your age (0 to 100+).

There are some nicknames that I have came across and I have said to myself "You got to be joking" and others I have said "You really want to be called that".

The next pages are for your enjoyment and fun. A disclaimer, I am not sure if anyone could list every nickname that is out there. My goal is not to say what is right or wrong nor truly understand why a certain nickname exist but for you to have a little fun and maybe think about an unusual nickname that exist among your friends, family or co-workers.

# Nick Names from A to Z

# A

# Nicknames that start with the Letter

# "A"

A.B., Abby, Able, Abnormal, Abu, AC, Ace, Acer, Aces, Acid Rain, Acorn, Admiral, Adrian, After Thought, African Delight, African Dream, African Storm, African Tiger, Afro,

Agape, Agent, Air, AJ, Aja, Ajax, AL, Alex, Algae, All-star, Alley Cat, Ally, Allegro, Almond, Almond Delight, Almond

Joy, Alpine, Alt, Ambassador, Amazin, Amazing, Amazon,

Amazon Queen, Ambition, Ambitious, Amigo, Amour,

Amy, Anchor, Andy, Angel, Angel Cake, Angel Eyes, Angle Light, Angel of Mine, Angel Pie, Angel Rock, Anger, Angie, Angie B, Animal, Anna, Annie, Answer, Ant, Antone, Anvil, Apache, Apache Rose, Ape, Ape-man, Apollo, Apple, Apple

Doe, Apple Dumpling, Apple Jack, Apple Jax, Apple Pie, Apple Plum, Apple Spice, Apricot, Apricot Spice, April,

April Mist, Aqua, Arcadia, Archer, Aries, Armed & Danger- ous, Arnie, Aroma, Arranger, Art, Artie, Ash, Ashy, Aspen, Assassin, Asterix, Asteroid, Astro, A-Train, Atom, Atomic, Atomic Dog, Attacker, Attila, Auto, Autumn, Ava, Aviator, Average Joe, Avenger, Avenging Angel, Avenging Warrior,

Awesome

**You may want to think twice if you call yourself** abnormal

**Apple Dumpling you are making me hungry**

**If you are a mean spirited person and you are not very liked, Angel may not be the best nickname**

# B

# Nicknames that start with the Letter

# "B"

B, Babe, Baby Boy, Baby Blue, Baby Breath, Baby Bottom,
Baby Cakes, Baby D, Baby Doll, Baby Dough, Baby Face,
Baby Girl, Baby Phat, Baby Sunshine, Babylicious, Bae, Baffler, Bagels,
Bake Bean, Baker, Ball, Ball Boy, Baller,
Bam, Bama, Bam Bam, Bambi, Bambino, Bank, Banky, Barb, Barber,
Barbie, Barn, Baron, Bart, Bashful, Basil,
Batboy, Batgirl, Batman, Battle Cat, Bazooka, B-Boy, BBQ, BC,
Beacon, Beaming, Beanie, Beanie Baby, Bear, Bearcat,
Beast, Beast Mode, Beatle, Beau, Beave, Beaver, Bebe, Bec, Bedrock,
Bee, Beef, Beef Stew, Beet, Bell, Bella,
Belle, Benji, Bennie, Benny, Bert, Beta, Beto, B-Fine, BG,
Big AL, Big Bank Hank, Big Bird, Big Boy, Big C, Big
Cat, Big Chief, Big Country, Big Daddy, Big Dogg, Big E,
Big Ern, Big Eyes, Big Ed, Big Guy, Big Hert, Big Hom- mie, Big Hurt,
Big Jake, Big Lou, Big Mac, Big Mama, Big Man, Big Mike, Big Moe,
Big O, Big Paulie, Big Perm, Big
Poppa, Big Sam, Big Show, Big Red, Big Rob, Big Thunder, Big Timer,
Big Willie, Big Worm, Biggie, Biggie-
Smalls, Bilal, Bilbo, Bill, Bingo, Binky, Bip, Bird, Bird
Man, Bit O'Honey, Bitsy, Bitsy Boo, Biz, Bizarre, BJ, BK,
B-Line, Black Corona, Black Diamond, Black Ice, Black
Leopard, Black Magic, Black Mamba, Black Panther,
Black Spice, Blacky, Blanket, Blass, Blaze, Bleak, Bleek,
Bless, Blimp, Blimpy, Blinded, Blinky, Blizz,
Block, Block Head, Blond Adonis, Blond Bear, Blondie,
Blond One, Blond Queen, Blond Tigress, Blossom, Blog,

Blood, Blue, Blue Eyes, Blue Money, Bluto, B-Nice, Bojan- gles, B-Moss, Bo, Bo Legs Bobo, Boiling Point, Bold, Bolt, Bombshell, Bomber, Bomper, Bone Crusher, Bones, Boney,

Boodle, Boomer, Boo, Boo Bear, Boo Boo, Booby, Boog, Boogaloo, Booger, Boogie, Book Worm, Booker, Book- man, Bookie, Boom Boom, Boomer, Boopy, Boostie, Boots, Booty, Bootsy, Bo Peep, Bo Pete, Bosco, Boss, Bossy, Bottomless, Bouncy, Bounty, Bow Wow, Box BoxTop, Boxer,

Boz, Braham Bull, Brain, Brandy, Brat, Bre, Bread Man,

Breakin Bad, B Real, Breezy, Bri, Brick, Brick House,

Bright Eyes, Brim, Britt, Broadway, B-Rod, Bron, Bronco, Bronx, Bronx Beast, Brow, Brown Eyes, Brown Bomber, Brownie, Bruiser, Bruno, Brute, Brutus, B-Smooth, Bub,

Bubba, Bubble Gum, Bubbles, Bubbly, Buck, Buck A Roo,

Bucket, Buckeye, Bucko, Buck Shot, Buck Wild, Bucky,

Bud, Buddha, Buddy, Buff, Buff Daddy, Buffy, Bug, Buga- bear, Bug Eye, Buggie Baby, Buggie Boo, Buggin, Buggin

Out, Buggy, Bugsy, Bull, Bull Whip, Bullet, Bullet Head,

Bulls Eye, Bumble, Bumble Bee, Bumbler, Bumper, Bumpkin, Bumpy, Bundles, Bundy, Bunkin, Bunky, Bunny, Bun- ny Bleu, Burr, Bopsy, Bus, Bush, Bushwhacker, Buster,

Butch, Butcher, Butler, Button, Butter Ball, Butterbean, But- ter Cup, Butter Milk, Butter Scotch, Butterfly, Buzz, Buzzard

If you are calling yourself Big Poppa or Biggie Smalls you must be on the verge of being one of the greatest Rappers of all time.

This nickname can have you mistaken as someone with very bad luck—86 year curse of the Boston Red Sox—Bambino

If you have this nickname and you are a little on the heavy side then people will think your name is a joke or a Antonym.—Bones

# C

# Nicknames that start with the Letter "C"

Cabby, Cacheton, Cactus Jack, Cadillac, Caesar, Cage, Cain, Cajun, Cakes, Cal, California Kid, Cally, Cam, Camel, Camelot, Cameo, Camera King, Camouflage, Candlestick Maker, Candi, Candy, Candy Man, Cannonball, Cap, Capone, Cappuccino, Cappy, Captain, Cardiac, Cardiac Kid, Cardinal Cal, Carebear, Caregiver, Caretaker, Carm, Car- mel, Carmel Dream, Carmel Delight, Carmel Spice, Carmel Wonder, Casanova, Cash, Cash-Money, Casper, Cat, Cat Daddy, Cat Eyes, Cat Quick, Cat Woman, Cautions, Caz, CC, C-Cat, Cease, Cedar, CeeCee, Cessna, Cha Cha, Chachis, Chae, Chago, Chainz, Chalo, Champ, Champaign, Chance, Charco, Charger, Charisma, Che, Charity, Charlie, Charm, Charmer, Charmin, Charming, Chase, Chato, Chavo, Chaz, Checkers, Checo, Cheeka, Cheeky, Cheery, Cheese, Cheese Head, Cheesy, Cheetah, Cheezen, Cheezy Mac, Chef, Chema, Chemo, Chenchi, Chente, Chepe, Cherokee, Cherub, Cherry, Cherry Drop, Chest, Chester, Chet, Chevy, Chica, Chicago, Chi Chi, Chick, Chickadee, Chicken, Chicken George, Chicky, Chiclets, Chico, Chief, Chief Rocker, Chill, Chili, Chilly, Chilo, Chimo, Chimpy, China, China Doll, Ching, Chingy, Chino, Chip, Chip Monk, Chipper, Chippy, Chipster, Chiquita, Chirpy, Choco-Lite, Chocolate, Chocolate Cherry, Chocolate Chip, Chocolate Chunk, Chocolate Dream, Chocolate Kiss, Chocolate Pie, Chocolate Swirl, Chocolate Thunder, Chocolate Tiger, Chocolate Twin, Choctaw, Choirboy,

Choo Choo, Choppa, Chrissie, Chubb, Chubby, Chuck, Chunky, Chuckles, Chuckster, Chui, Chulado, Chump,

Chumpy, Chunky Charles, Chuy, CiCi, Cider, Cinco, Cinnamon, Cinnamon Buz, Cisco, CJ, Clanky, Classified, Classy,

Classy Lady, Clay, Cleo, Cleveland, Cliff, Cliffy, Clipper,

Clipper Boy, Clipse, Clout, Clover, Clubber, Clumpy, Clumsy, C-More, C Note, Coal, Coal House, Coat, Cobra, Cochese, Cocky, Coco, Coconut, Coco Puffs, Coffee, Cold,

Cold Blooded, Comfort, Comforter, Commander, Concha, Concho, Cochotas, Condor, Confetti, Contribution, Coffee,

Coffee Brown, Coffee & Cream, Coke, Coke Bottle,

Cooch, Cook, Cookie, Cookie Crumble, Cookie Monster,

Cool, Cool Breeze, Cool Papa, Cooney, Coop, Cork, Corky, Corn, Cornbread, Corona, Corrupt, Cosmo, Cotton, Cotton

Ball, Cotton Butt, Cotton Mouth, Couch, Couch Potato,

Cougar, Count, Cousin, Cover Girl, Covey, Cowboy, Cowboy Black, Cowgirl, Coyote, Coz, Crabby, Cracker Jack,

Crane man, Crash, Crazy, Crazy Legs, Cream, Creamy, Creator, Crème Soda, Creole, Cricket, Crime Dawg, Crime

Dogg, Crimpy, Crimson, Cringle, Crip, Crisco, Crisp,

Crispy, Crissy, Crucial, Cruiser, Crump, Crush,

Crusher, Crusty, Cruz, Crybaby, Crystal, Crystal Delight,

Crystal Lite, Crystal Water, C-Smooth, Cubbie, Cubbie

Bear, Cubbly, Cuddle Bear, Cuddle Bunny, Cuddly Wuddly,

Cujo, Cup Cake, Cupid, Curious, Curley, Current, Cushy

Butt, Custer, Custodian, Custom, Custom Design, Cut, Cut- ie, Cutie

Patootie, Cutie Pie, Cutty, Cuz, Cyclone, Czar

When I see this nickname I envision someone always wearing a cowboy hat and cowboy boots.—Cowboy

Crime Dogg or Crime Dawg—Either you are McGruff or Fred McGriff. Both bring high standards that may be tough to match.

A friendly ghost? Now how do you explain to others why you should be called Casper.

# D

# Nicknames that start with the Letter "D"

DaDa, Dabadguy, Dabby, Daddy, Daddy Mack, Daddy
Rich, Dae Dae, Daffodil, Daffy, DaFuture, Dago, Dah, Daisy, DaJet,
Dak, DaKing, Dakota, Dakota Red, Dandy,
Dancin Don, Dangerous, Dangerous One, Dangles, Dank,
Dano, Dapper, Dapper Dave, Darby, Dare Devil, Dark
Avenger, Dark Chocolate, Dark Knight, Dark & Lovely, Dark Man,
Dark Side, Darling, Dash, Dasher, Dat Hoppa, Davey, Dawg, Dax,
Daze, Dazzle, Dazz, Dazzy, Deacon, Dead Eye, Dean, DB, Deb,
Debbie, Debo, Dee, Dee Dee,
Déjà, Déjà Vu, Del, Delicious, Delta, Demon, Demon Hook,
Denji, Dennis the Menace, Denny, Denver, Derk, Derky,
Destiny, Desire, Deuce, Devilin, Devious, Dew Drop,
Dezzy, Diamond, Diaz, Dibble, Diddle, Diddly Doo, Diego,
Diesel, Dig, Digby, Digger, Diggs, Diggy, Digum, Dill,
Dime, Dime Piece, Dimes, Dimples, Dimply Divine, Dina,
Dinky, Dino, Dip, Dippy, Dipsy, Dirk, Dirty, Dirty Dan,
Dirty Blonde, Dirty One, Dirty Red, Dish, Dish Head, Ditsy,
Ditto, Dixie, Dixie Chick, Diva, Diva Doll, Divine, Dizzy, DJ, Dk,
D-Nice, Dobby, Doc, Doc Holloway, Docker, Doctor, Doctor Feel
Good, Dodger, Doe, Doggy, Doll, Doll
Face, Dollar, Dollar Bill, Dolly, Dome, Dominant, Domino,
Don, Don Juan, Donnie, Donut, Dooby, Doodle, Doodle
Bug, Doogie, Dope, Dopy, Dora, Dorito, Dorky, Dot, Double Barrel,
Double D, Double Mint, Double O, Dough Boy, Douser, Dove,
Downtown, DP, Dra, Dragon, Drake, Drama Dramadic, Drama

Queen, Drano, D-Ray, Dr. Jekyll, Dr. Who, Dr. Dre, Dre, Dread Head, Dreak, Dream, Dreamer,

Dream Maker, Dream Snatcher, Drew, Drifter, Drizzle, Drizzy, Droopy, D-Train, Ducci, Duchess Duck, Duck Boy, Duck Mouth, Ducked Off, Duckie, Ducky, Dude, Dudy, Duffy, Duggard, Duggin, Duggy, Duke, Dumpling, Dumpy, Dungy, Dunkin, Duo, Durk, Dustin, Dusty, Dutch, Dwarf, Dyme, Dynamic, Dynamite, Dynamo, Dynasty, Dyno,

This nickname was developed by my daughter regarding my youngest son. His name is Ben and our goal was to call him Benji but my daughter at the time (Age 4) could not quite get the B sound and she began to call him Denji and it stuck.

For those who have decided to use this nickname you better be as tough as Debo from Ice Cube's movie "Friday"

Diamond—What a very pricey nickname.

E

# Nicknames that start with the Letter

## "E"

Eagle, Eagle Claw, Eagle Eye, Eagle Point, Ears, Easy, Easy on the Eyes, Eazy, Ebony, Ebony Doll, Ebony Dream, Ebony Eyes, Ebony Kiss, Ebony One, Ebony Rose, Ebony

Shadow, Eclipse, Ecstasy, Ed, Edge, Edgy, Eel, Egg, Egg Drop, Egg Head, Ego, Eight-Ball, EJ, EL, Eldorado, Elite,

Elk, Elkin, Elmo, Elusive, E-man, Emerald, Emmy, Emperor, Empire, Enchanted, Enchanting One, Encore, Endless, Enemy, Enemy Within, Energizer, Enormous, Enough, Envision, Epic, Ernie, Eros, Erroneous, Erv, Esquire, Essence,

Esteem, Etta, Etch, Euro, Evap, Eventful, Everlast, Evidence, Evolve, Exchange, Exciting, Exclusive, Executive,

Exhibit, Exquisite, Ex Why Zee, Extraordinary, Eye Candy, Eyes, EZ

With a nick name like Executive. You better be large and in charge!!!!!

Egg Head—I have
been called that
before in my lifetime.
Never wanted it as
a nickname

Those individuals with the nickname of Easy, I hope you are very laid back and easy to talk to.

Nicknames that start with the Letter

F

# F

# Nicknames that start with the Letter

## "F"

Fab, Fabulous, Fairy, Fairy One, Faith, Falco, Falcon, Fallen Angel, Fam, Fancy, Fancy Fawn, Fa'ness, Fannie, Fantastic, Fantasy, Fashion, Fat Daddy, Fat Boy, Fat Jaws, Fat Man, Fate, Fat Fat, Fatso, Fay Fay, Fe Fe, Feather, Feather Fanny, Feature, Felix, Fellow, Fern, Ferocious, Ferrari, Festive, Festus, Fetty, Fiddler, Fidget, Fido, Fig, Figgy, Fig Newton, Fike, Fike Dog, Filly, Fin, Finnie, Fink, Fire, Firecracker, Fireman, Firm, Fish, Fit, Fitty, Fitz, Fizz, Flamboyant, Flame, Flamer, Flame Thrower, Flare, Flash, Flat Top, Flap Jack, Flappy, Flavor, Flawless, Flea, Fleet, Fletch, Flex, Flip, Flipper, Flippy, Flo, Flock, Flock a Flame, Flod, Flodo, Floppy, Flopsy, Flower, Fluffy, Flurry, Flusher, Fly, Fly Guy, Flyte, FM, Focal, Focus, Fog, Fonda. Fondler, Fonzie, Foo Foo, Foots, Footsie, Forest, Formula, Fortune, Fortu- nate, Forty, Four Runner, Fox, Foxy, Fozy Bear, Fozzy, Franchise, Frankie, Frat, Freak, Freckles, Free, Free bird, Freeze, Freight Train, French, Frenchy, Fresca, Fresh, Fridge, Friend, Frisco, Frisky, Fritz, Fro, Frog, Froggy, Frogman, Frost, Frosty, Fruity, Fruity Loom, Fruity Pebbles, Fudge, Fudgy, Fuego, Fufu, Fundamentals, Funkmaster, Funky, Funny Bunny, Furious, Future, Futuristic, Future Shock, Fuzzy, Fuzzy Bear, Fuzzy Bunny, Fuzzy Wuzzy,

Fireman—I did not verify the occupation of those who are calling themselves Fireman. I do hope they are a fire fighter

Flap Jack is another interesting nickname. I am not sure but maybe the person got this nickname because they like to eat flap jacks?

Flipper or Fish? Maybe you were inspired by the sitcom Barney Miller and Abe Vigoda as Detective Fish was your favorite character or maybe you were inspired by that other TV show that starred dolphin named Flipper. But then again maybe I am showing my age.

G

# Nicknames that start with the Letter

## "G"

Gabby, Gabe, Gabi, Gadget, Galaxy, Gam Gam, Game,
Gamegreen, Gangrene, Gangly, Gap, Gap Tooth, Gator,
Gay, Gazelle, G-Baby, Gee, Geechy, Geese, Gel, Gem, Genie, Gentle,
Geronimo, Gent, Ghost, Ghost Dancer, Ghost Face, Gib, Gibbo, Gibby,
Giddy, Gifted, GiGi, Giggle Bear,
Giggle Bunny, Giggles, Giggly, Gilligan, Gimp, Gimpy,
Ginger Bread, Ginger Snap, Ginger Spice, Gino, Gip, Gipper, Girly,
Gizmo, Gizzard, Gladiator, Glamour, Glass,
Glassy, Glaze, Glazzy, Glide, Glitzy, Glizzy, Glory, Glove, Glow,
G-Man, G-Money, Goat, God Got Me, Goddess, Gofer, Go Go, Gold,
Golden, Golden Apple, Golden Boy,
Golden Flake, Golden Greek, Golden Knight, Goldie, Golf Guy,
Goliath, Golly, Gomer, Gonzo, Goggles, Good Look- ing, Goof, Goofy,
Googs, Goon, Gooney, Goose, Gopher,
Gorgeous, Gorilla, Gosie Goose, Gotti, Grace, Gracie,
Grady, Gramps, Grams, Grand Pooh-Bah, Granite, Granny,
Grape Ape, Grape Juice, Grasshopper, Grassy, Gravy,
Greaser, Greasy, Gree, Greek, Green Eyes, Green Guy,
Greeny, Grey, Grey Goose, Greyhound, Grey Matter, Griff, Griggs,
Grimy, Grin, Gringo, Grip, Gripper, Grippin, Grit, Grizzle, Grizzly,
Gromo, Gronk, Groove, Grouchy, Gruff, Gruncho, Grungy, Grunter,
Gucci, Gulf, Gulf Man, Gully,
Gum Drop, Gumby, Gummy, Gump, Guru, Gus, Gusto,
Gusty, Gym Rat, Gypsy, Gza

Grasshopper—Can anyone say Kung Fu

When I think of someone with the nickname of
Gizmo—I think of a very technically smart
person. I hope you fit that characterization. If
not then maybe you could be from the movie
Gremlins—Gizmo

If you have this nickname then it must refer to
the eyewear that you have—
Goggles

# H

# Nicknames that start with the Letter "H"

Hack, Hacksaw, Hairy, Hal, Half-Pint, Ham, Hambone,
Hamburger, Hammer, Hamp, Handsome, Handy Man,
Hangman, Hank, Hanky, Happy, Happy Jack, Happy One, Hardcore,
Hardwood, Harlem, Harley, Harp, Harry, Hart,
Hatchet, Haven, Havoc, Hawaiian Honey, Hawk, Hawk
Eye, Haze, Hazel, Hazy, Head, Head Hunter, Heart of Gold,
Heath, Heavenly, Heavy D, Heavy Load, Heckle, Helicopter, Hell Cat,
Hell Raiser, Hennessey, Henry Boy, Herb,
Herby, Herc, Hercules, Hero, Hershey, Hershey Kiss, Hershey Lover,
Hick, Hickory, Highlander, High Lite, High
Standard, High Top, Hill, Hinky, Hippie, Hippo, Hit Man,
Hoagie, Hobbit, Hobby, Hobo, Hocus, Hodges, Hodgie, Hodo, Hog
Wild, Hogan, Hoggin, HoJo, Hola, Holly, Hollywood, Homeboy,
Home Girl, Homie, Hondo, Honey, Honey
Badger, Honey Bun, Honey Bunch, Honey Bunny, Honey Dew, Honey
Dipper, Honey Mellon, Honey Pie, Hoodie,
Hook, Hoot, Hootie, Hoover, Hop, Hope, Horse, Hoss, Hot, Hot n
Spicy, Hot Rod, Hot Shot, Hot Stuff, Houdini, Hour Glass, House,
House Pipe, Houser, Houston, Howie, Howler, Huckleberry, Huey,
Huff, Huggy Buggy, Hugh, Hugo, Hula, Hulk, Hucksters, Human
Tornado, Hummer, Hun,
Hunter, Hurricane, HurriKane, Hurt, Hush, Hustle, Hustle
Man

If you are using this nick name, I hope your physical look matches the name. Hercules, Hercules,
Hercules

This is one of my favorites. It was a nickname that my uncles gave to a gentleman who visited a lady next door to them in Little Rock, AR. They stated that his vehicle did not have an exhaust pipe but a chimney pipe that he had gotten off of the house. His nickname was
House Pipe

If this is your nickname then I am going to assume you carry a lot of sweetness in a nice small package—Hershey Kiss

# Nicknames that start with the Letter

## "I"

Ice, Ice Cream, Ice Cube, Ice Man, Ice Pick, Icing, Icky, Icy,
Icy Hot, Icy Rosebud, Iggy, Igor, Ika, Ike, Ill, Imagine, I- Max,
Immortal, Imp, In to Me, Inca, Indestructible, India,
Indian, Indigo, Indigo Rose, Indo, Infamous, Inferno, Inferno Kidd,
Infinity, Indy, Inky, Innocence, Innovator, Insane, Inside Man, Intel,
Intelligent, Intentional, Intentional Lover,
Intro, Intruder, Invincible, Invisible Man, Inviting, Irish,
Iron, Iron Head, Ironman, Iron Mike, Isis, IT, Itsy Bitsy, Itty
Bitty, Ivan, Ivan the Terrible, Ivory, Ivory Dream, Ivory
Tower, Ivy, Izo, Izzy

Ice Cube—Really? You are calling yourself Ice Cube!!!! No way!!!

NWA, Friday, Friday After Next,
Are We there Yet?,
Boys in the Hood, Barbershop
Doughboy, Amerikkka Most Wanted

Hopefully you can live up to this type of notoriety!!!!

Ironman—Unless you have the power of a marvel character or have the ability to run a marathon, swim 2.6 miles and ride a bike 112 miles, - You may want to stay away from this nickname

J

# Nicknames that start with the Letter "J"

Jack, Jacko, Jack Rabbit, Jada, Jade, Jaguar, Jake, Jalapeno
John, Jam Jam Jam, Jamie, Jammy, Jammy Pie, Jan, Janay,
Jar Head, Jasmine, Jasper, Java, Jay, Jay Bird, Jay Jay, Jazz, Jazzman,
Jazzy, JB, J Bug, JC, JD, Jeannie, Jeb, Jeezy, Jelly, Jelly Bean, Jelly Roll,
Jen, Jenna, Jenny, Jep Jep, Jersey Joe,
Jesse, Jester, Jet, Jeter, Jewel, Jigga, Jiggity Jam, Jif, Jiffy, Jigsaw, Jigsy,
Jimbo, Jim Bob, Jingles, Jingo, Jinx, Jitter- bug, Jitters, Jizzle, JJ, Jo, Jock,
Jocko, Jocky, Jodi, Jody,
Joe, Joey, John, Johnny, JoJo, Joker, Jolly, Joltin, Jon Jon,
Jookie, Josh, Jouster, Joy, Joyrider, JP, J-Rock, JR, JT,
Juango, Jubble, Jubilee, Judge, Judo, Jug, Jugger Knot, Jug
Head, Juggler, Juice, Juicy, Juicy Fruit, JuJu, Jules, Julie,
Jumbo, Jumper, Jumpin Jack, Jumpy, June, June bug, Junior, Junk
Master, Juno, Jupiter, Justice, Juvenile, JV

There is nothing like have a refreshing
piece of gum—Juicy fruit

If you have the nickname of this I
salute you for your service to the
country—
Jarhead

Jug head—How many of you all think about the
Archies when you hear that nickname.

# Nicknames that start with the Letter

# "K"

Kay Gee, Kandi Kane, Kane, Kanga, Kango, Kano, Kansas City, Kappy, Karm, Karma, Karo Sweet, Kat, Kay Kay, Kay Jay, Kaylo, KB, KC, KD, Kee Kee, Keg Man, Keidy, Kel, Kelly, Ken, Keno, Kentucky, Kermit, Kev, Kez, KG, Khaki Jack, Khan, Kia, Kibble, Kid, Kiddo, Kike, KiKi, Killa, Killer, Killer B, Kilo, Kilroy, Kim, Kimble, Kimmy, King, King Buck, King Cobra, King Kong, King Tim, King Tut,

Kip, Kipper, Kipster, Kirb, Kirby, kirbster, Kiss, Kite Flyer, Kit Kat, Kitten, Kitty, Kitty Boy, Kitty Hawk, Kitty Kat, Kiwi, Kiwi Sweet, Kix, Kizzy, Klassified, Klay, Knees,

Knight, Knobby, Knockout, Knuckles, Kochiese, Kodak, Koffee, Koffee Brown, KoKo, Kold Blooded, Kommander, Konk, Kool, Koop, Kracker, Krash, Krazy Karl, Krispy, Kristie, Krusher, Kryptonite, Krystal, KT, Kush, Kup, Kurupt, Kurious, KV

Kiwi sounds like a delicious refreshing name. Does
your personality match it?

I am not sure what to say on this one.
Maybe you were a great young king or you are
just a history buff—King Tut

If you have this nickname I hope it is because you are
very good boxer or a gorgeous person? -
Knock Out

# L

# Nicknames that start with the Letter

## "L"

LA, La La, Lace, Lacy, Lady, Lady Bug, Lady Di, Lady
Luck, Lady Giant, Lady T, Laffy Taffy, Lake, Lake Love, Lala, Lalo,
Lama, Lamb, Lamp, Lanky, Lap Dog, Lappy,
Laredo, Large n Charge, Lats, Lava Kid, Lawman, Lay Lay,
Laya, Layla, Lays, Lazy, Lazy Eye, Lazy Lou, LB, Lea,
Leafa, Leaper, Leaping, Ledger, Lee Lee, Left Eye, Lefty, Legacy,
Legatron, Legend, Leggy, Lego, Legs, Lem, Lemon, Lemon Drop,
Lemon Head, Lemon Lime, Lemon Spice,
Len, Lenny, Leo, Leopard, Lethal, Lethal Weapon, Levi,
Lex, Lexy, Liberty, Liberty Lady, Libra, Licorice, Licorice Stick,
Lightening, Lightening Bolt, Lightening Strike, Lil Auntie, Lil Bear,
Lil BeBe, Lil Bit, Lil Bootsie, Lil Dude, Lil Earl, Lil Fiz, Lil Mama, Lil
Man, Lil Rod, Lil Tim, Lil
Uncle, Lil Willie, Lil Zane, Lillie, Lillie Pad, Limelight,
Limon, Liquid, Little Bear, Little Boy Blue, Little Joe, Little
Lady, Little One, Lima Bean, Limy, Lincoln, Lion, Lion
Heart, Lippy, Livindahighlife, Living Legend, Liz, Lizzard, Lizzy, LL,
Lobo, Locket, Loco, Logic, Logo, Lojack, Lola,
Lollie,
Lolo, Lon, Londo, London, Lone Wolf, Long, Lonzo, Loner,
Lonesome, Loney, Loon Lonnie, Looney, Looney Tooney,
Loopy, Loose, Loose Booty, Loosie Goosy, Loots, Lopy, Louie, Lovable,
Love Muffin, Lovely, Lover Boy, Lovey, Lovey Dovey, Low Down, Low
Voltage, L Roc, LT, Lucy Goosy, Lulu, Lucky, Lucky Charm, Lucky
Lennie, Lucho, Lucky Star, Lucy, Ludwig, Luigi, Lulu, Lumpkin, Lumpy,
Lunatic, Lupe, Lurch, Luscious, Luvbug, LV, Lyte

I do get it. Your name is Diane. But to call yourself
Lady Di????

If you have this
nickname can you
really change your |
spots- Leopard

Just maybe this was a great vegetable delight that
you could not get enough of. I hope that is the
case.
—Lima Bean

# Nicknames that start with the Letter "M"

Ma, Mac, Mack Daddy, Macy, Maddy, Mad Dog, Mad-Max,
Mad Mike, Maddi, Mafisto, Magic, Magician, Magic Man, Magnificent,
Mahogany, Mailman, Main, Major, Makin the
Bacon, Mamba, Man Child, Mane, Maniac, Manly, Man
Man, Manny, Mantan, Maple, Maple, Maple Sweet, Marathon Man,
Marcy, Marge, Margi, Margo, Mango Sweet, Mario, Marley, Mars,
Marshmallow, Marvelous, Mase,
Master, Mate, Matrix, Matt, Mauler, Maverick, Max, May, May May,
Maz, MC, Meadow, Meat Head, Meaty, Medicine Man, Meek, Meg,
Megabucks, Megaman, Megatron, Meezy, Mel, Mellow, Mellow Yellow.
Melo, Melon Tart,
Memphis, Menage, Mercedes, Mercury, Merl, Merlin,
Method, Metro, Mick, Mickey, Micro, Middle Man, Midget, Midnight,
Miff, Miffy, Mighty Mouse, Mighty One, Mighty
T, Mike-Mike, Mikey, Mile High, Miles, Millie, Milken, Milkman,
Milky, Milky Way, Milo, MiMi, Mind Spring, Mindy, Mini Me,
Minnie, Minitron, Minty, Minty Fresh,
Miracle, Misery, Mislead, Miss Diva, Miss Fitness, Missing
Link, Missy, Mister, Mister Cee, Misty, Misty Blue, Misty
Eyes,
Misty Water, Misunderstood, Mix Master, Mo, Mob, Mobile
One, Mocha, Model, Molasses, Molly, Moochie, Moogie,
Moe, Mongo, Monk, Monkey, Monkey Man, Momee, Momo,
Monarch, Mond, Money, Mongoose, Monster, Monster Mash, Monty,
Mookie, Moon, Moonie, Moose, Moosy, Mop
Head, Mopsy, Moses, Mountain Man, Mouse, Mouser,

Mousy, Movie Star, Mozart, Mr. Big, Mr. Big Stuff, Mr. Ed, Mr. Hyde, Mr. Magoo, Mr. Opinion, Mr. Spectacular, Mr. Tibbs, Mr. Wonderful, Ms Chunky, Ms Mocha, Ms Thang, Ms Thing, Muddy, Muddy Water, Mufasa, Muffin, Muffin Top, Muffy, Mugsy, Mull, Mullet, Mumbles, Munckin, Muncho, Munchy, Muneco, Muppet, Murph, Murphy, Mush, Mushy, Mustang, Mustang Girl, Mustard, Mutiny, Mystery, Mysterious, Mystic, Mystical, Mystro, Myth, Myzery, Mz Dark, Mz Thickness,

Mad Dog—This is probably one tough person.

If you have this nickname you better be a heck
of a pilot or a trailblazer.-
Maverick

I am pretty sure if this is your nickname that there is
a good reason for it. You could be a star or someone
believes that you should be in the movies. - Movie Star

So we are half way through the alphabet and so far our breakdown is as follows:

**Letter A (113) Letter B (307)**

**Letter C (301) Letter D (211)**

**Letter E (78) Letter F (150)**

**Letter G (152) Letter H (128)**

**Letter I (64)**

**Letter J (112) Letter K (101)**

**Letter L (161) Letter M (201)**

Deserts, Cities, Animals, Angels and Fruit all make up some of the interesting nicknames in the first half of our list. A to M nicknames consist of 2,079 different nicknames with the letters B (307) and C (301) making up almost 30% (29.2%) of the total. Let's now explore N thru Z.

# Nicknames that start with the Letter

# "N"

Nabisco, Nails, Na Na, Nacho, Nah Nah, Nana, Nancazz,
Nando, Napoleon, Nappy, Nas, Nash, Nasty, Nate, Natural,
Naughty, Nature, Nature Boy, Navajo, Nay, Nebo, Neck, Neckbone,
Ned, Needle, Needy, Negatron, Neka, Neko,
Nelly, Nembo, Neo, Neon Leon, Neon Man, Neor, Neptune,
Nero, Nessa, Nette, Nevada, Never Nervous, New Beginning, New
Hope, New York, Nia, Niagara, Nibbles, Nicety, Nick, Nicko, Nickel,
Nicky, Niecy, Nifty, Nik Nik, Nikka,
Nikkei, Ninja, Nina, Niner, Nino, Nipper, Nisha, Nita, Nitro, Nitt,
Nitty, N-Joy, Noel, NOLA Boy, Nomo, Norm, Noodle,
Noodles, Nookie, Nora, Norm, Nose, Nosey, Nothing But the Best,
Notorious, N-Spire, Nugget, # Six, Numero Uno,
NuNu, Nutmeg, Nut Cracker, Nuts, Nutso, Nutty, Nutty
Buddy,

New York—Hopefully you are from the big apple or you are from the 11th state of the these United
States

Pretty cheap
nickname but quite
a few of these does add
up—Nickel

NEO—I really do hope you are the one..

# Nicknames that start with the Letter "O"

O, Oak, Oasis, Obi Wan, Obo, Obsession, O.C., Ocean,
Ocho, Octo, October, O.D., Odd Ball, Oddly, Odessa, Odin,
Odyssey, Official, O.G., Oil Can, Olive Oil, Oily, O.J.,
Okie, Oklahoma, Okra, Old Man, Old School, Ollie, Olympus, Omar,
Omega, Omega Dragon, On A Mission, On My Own, On the One,
Once in a Life Time, One Way, One for the Road, One in A Million,
One Time, One Way, Once, Onex, Onion, Onion Head, Onion
Bottom, Ooze, Opal, Open Sesame, Opey, Opium, Orange, Orange
Peel, Orator, Orca,
Orchard, Oreo, Orion, Oscar, OT, Othello, Otis, Otto,
Ounce, Ouster, Outlaw, Oval, Oven Fresh, Owned, Ox, OZ,
OZO

Omega —I gather you consider yourself last, love the Greek Alphabet or in a fraternity.

Maybe you got this nickname because you love that delicious taste.—Oreo

# P

# Nicknames that start with the Letter "P"

Pablo, Pacific, Paco, Pain, Pal, Pancho, Panda, Panky, Pansy, Pansly, Panther, Papa, Papi, Pappy, Patriot, Passion,

Pasty, Pat, Pattie, Patty Melt, Pauli, Paws, Peaches, Peach Pie, Peachy, Peachy Peacock, Peachy Pearl, Peachy Pie,

Peanut Butter, Pie, Peanut, Pearl, Pearly, Pebbles, Pec, Peek a Boo, Peewee, Pedro, Peg, Peggy, Peggy Sue, Penguin, Penny, Penny Loafer, Penny Lover, Penny Rein, Pepper, Pepper Jack, Peppermint Patty, Percy, Perky, Pete, Peter

Piper, Pettie, Phantom, Pharaoh, Phenomenon, Philly, Phocus, Phoenix, Pickle, Pickly, Picture Perfect, Pie, Piggy, Piglet, Pilaf, Pilgrim, Pill, Pillow, Pillow Talk, Pin Cushion,

Pinch, Pincher, Pine Cone, Pinky, Pinky Pie, Pipe, Pipe Fitter, Pipe N Hot, Pippy, Pirate, Pistol, Pit-bull, Pixie, Pizza, PJ, Plastic Man, Platinum, Play, Playful, Pleaser, Pleasure, Plower, Plow Boy, Plum, Plum Dumplin, Plumber, Plump, Plumpkin, Plumplicious, Plumps, Plumpy, Plumy. Plunger,

Plush, Plush Bear, Plush Bunny, Plushness, Pluto, P-Mooney, Pocket, Poco, Poetry, Pogo, Point,

Pointless, Poky, Polar, Polar Bear, Polish, Polly, Polo, Poncho, Pontiac, Poochie, Pooh, Pooh Bear, Pook, Pookie, Pookums, Poopy, Pooty, Popeye, Pop, Popcorn, Poppy,

Pops, Porche, Pork Chop, Porky, Posey, Positive, Pot Head, Pouchie, Pound, Potty, Prancer, Preach, Preacher, Precious,

Precious Doll, Precious Love, Predator, Preferred Stock, Pretender, Pretty Boy, Pretty Ricky, Pretty Tony, Preview, Priceless, Prickly, Pride, Pride of the South, Prima, Primetime, Prince, Prince Charming, Princess, Pringle, Prissy, Prodigy, Professor, Psycho, Psycho Path, Puck, Puddin, Pudding Pop, Puddy, Pudge, Pudgy, Puffy, Puffy Bottom, Pumpkin, Pun, Punisher, Punk, Punkin, Punkin Wunkin, Punky, Puny, Pup, Puppy Love, Pure, Pusha, Pzaz

I am the wonder, I am a wee, I am known as P
Mooney. I seen someone with this nickname and all I
could think about was being in the first grade in 1972
and seeing this puppet named P Mooney. Strange
nickname to have.




Either you are the next Deon
Sanders or you are always around at a special time—
Primetime




Panda—I am either thinking Chinese
food or a nice cuddly bear.

# Nicknames that start with the Letter

## "Q"

Q, Q-Ball, QC, Q-Dog, Q-Pop, Qeasha, Q-Note, QT, Q-Tip,
Quaalude, Quack, Quacker, Quack Master, Quad, Quail,
Quaker, Quam, Quan, Quana, Quarter, Quasar, Que,
Quench, Queen, Queen Bee, Queenie, Quent, Quest, Question,
Question Mark, Quick, Quick Draw, Quickness,
Quinn, Quint, Quite Storm, Quitman, Quiver, Quiz, Quiz- mo, Qwel

Twenty-five cents, one -fourth of a mile, fifteen minutes before or after the hour—Not sure but there has to be a reason to have this nickname.—Quarter

Q-Tip—Either you have something to do with one of the best known cotton swab or you are a prolific rapper

# R

# Nicknames that start with the Letter

# "R"

Rabbit, Racer, Radar, Radio, Rae Rae, Raff, Rage, Rags,
Raheem, Rain, Rainbow, Rain Man, Rainey, Raj, Ram, Ram Rod,
Rambler, Ramblin, Rambo, Rampage, Range, Ranger, Ranky, Ransom,
Rapid Delivery, Rascal, Rat, Raven, Ravishing, Ray Ray, Razor, Razz,
R&B, RB, RC, Real Deal,
Real One, Rean, Reaper, Rebel, Rebellious, Reckless, Red,
Red Barron, Red Dog, Red Hound, Redeemer, Redman,
Reese's, Reese's Cup, Reflex, Reg, Regal, Ree Ree, Reignman, Remy,
Ren, Rennie, Reno, Reo, Resolution, Restless, Retta, Revelation, Rex,
Rhino, Rhino Tough, Rich, Richie, Richie Rich, Rick, Rickie, Rico,
Rico Suave, Riddle, Riddler, Rider, Right on Time, Ringmaster, Ringo,
Rio, Rip,
Ripper,
Ripples, Rising Sun, Rista, Rizzo, RJ, Ro, Rob, Robbie,
Robbo, Robin, Rojo, Rob Roy, Roc, Rocco, Rock, Rocket,
Rock On, Rockin Robin, Rock Star, Rockwood, Rocky, Rod, Rod Dog,
Rod Man, Rodeo, Rodzilla, Rojo, Rolex,
Rollie, Rollie Pollie, Rollin, Rolo, Roman, Rome, Romeo, Romy, Rona,
Roney, Ronnie, Roo, Rookie, Rope Man, Ro
Ro, Roscoe, Rose, Rosey, Rotten, Rough Rider, Roughy,
Rough Rover, Rowdy, Roxy, Royal, Royal Duchess, Royalty, Royce,
Roz, RR, RT, Ruby, Ruckus, Rudd, Rudolph, Rudy, Ruff, Ruffin,
Rugged, Rug Rat, Rum, Rum Cake,
Run, Runner, Running Man, Rupert, Rusty,

When I hear this nickname, I am not sure if this is someone who was a big Arnold Schwarzenegger fan or someone who love doing a very popular dance from the 90's.—Running Man

With this nickname you could be one very sharp person—Razor

I had a class mate with this nickname back in middle school and it was not inspired by the movie. However this nickname could mean you are a boxer or have a good pal named Bullwinkle.
—Rocky

# S

# Nicknames that start with the Letter "S"

Sable, Sabo, Sabra, Sacred, Sadie, Safety Man, Sage, Saggy,
Sahara, Sailor, Sal, Sally, Salsa, Salty, Sammy, Samsonite, Sand, Sandy,
Sandman, Sap, Sapphire, Sarge, Sasha, Sassy,
Satch, Satin, Satin Doll, Satin Sensation, Saturn, Sausage
Maker, Savage, Savana, Savory, Savory Sensation, Sax, Sax
Man, Saxon, Scar, Scarface, Scarecrow, Scarlet, Schmidty,
Schoolboy, Scientific, Scooby, Scooby Doo, Scoop, Scoops,
Scoot, Scooter, Scooty Booty, Scotty, Score, Scorpion,
Scout, Scrap Iron, Scrappy, Scrappy Doo, Scratch, Scribe,
Scribbles, Scrub, Scrumptious, Sea Biscuit, Sea Otter, Senator, Secret,
Self-Made, Sensation, Sensational, Serge, Sergio, Seth, Seven, Shade,
Shades of Grey, Shady, Shady B,
Shady P, Shady T, Shadow, Shadow Boxer, Shadow Dancer, Shag,
Shaggy, Shamrock, Shambina Shame, Shane,
Shank, Shark, Shasta, Shawty, Shay, Shay Shay, Shea, Sheba, Shell,
Shelly, Sheed, Sheena, Sheik, Sherriff, Shep, Ship, Shiver, Shock, Shock
G, Shocka, Shocker, Shoeless, Shoes,
Shooter, Short Cake, Short Stuff, Shorty, Showboat, Show
Me the Money, Show Stopper, Shug, Shump, Siddy, Sil, Silk, Silky, Silky
One, Silky Smooth, Silky Shine, Silky
Water, Silly, Silly Willy, Silver, Simba. Simmy, Sinister, Sir Charles, Sir
Kev, Sir Lancelot, Sir Rodney, Six-Nine, Sister,
Sizzle, Sizzler,
Skeeter, Skillet, Skimpy, Skip, Skipper, Skippy, Skittles,
Skuta, Sky, Skyla, Skylark, Sky Scrapper, Skywalker, Slant, Slate, Slayer,
Sleepy, Sleepy Head, Slice, Slick, Slick Rick,

Slim, Slim Diva, Slimy, Sling, Slip, Slippery, Slippy,
Slouchy, Slow Poke, Slug, Slugger, Slush Puppy, Sluchy,
Sly, Smalls, Smarty, Smiles, Smiley, Smoke, Smokey, Smokin, Smoochie,
Smoopy, Smoors, Smooth, Smooth Chocolate, Smooth Operator,
Smumpkin, Smush, Snap, Snapper, Sneaky, Snicker, Sniffy, Snip,
Sniper, Snipple,
Snipps, Snookems, Snookerpooh, Snooky, Snoop, Snoopy,
Snooty, Snooze, Snoozer, Snorkel, Snow, Snow Bunny,
Snowflake, Snow White, Snuffy, Snuggabug, Snuggle Bun- ny, Snuggles,
Snuggy, Snuggy Bear, Snugly, Sockeye,
Socks, Sodbuster, Solar, Soldier, Sole, Solid Man, Sonny,
Sonic, Soul Chief, Soul Man, Southern Bell, Southern Gentleman,
Southern Style, Southpaw, Space, Space Cowboy,
Spark, Spark Plug, Sparkle, Sparky, Spartan, Spearmint,
Special Delivery, Special K, Spectacles, Speckles, Speed,
Speed Demon, Speedy, Speedy Gonzales, Spice, Spice Girl,
Spice One, Spicy, Spider, Spike, Spike D, Spiffy, Spike,
Spin, Spindarella, Spinner, Spin Top, Spirit, Spirit Doctor,
Spirit Within, Spitfire, Splash, Splendid, Spo, Spooky,
Spongy, Sponsor, Spoony, Sport,
Sporty, Spot, Sprout, Squiggles, Sprinter, Sprite, Spud,
Spunky, Sputnik, Square, Squeally, Squeaker, Squeaky,
Squirrel, Squirt, Squishy, Stacks, Stallion, Stank, Star, Star Bright,
Stardust, Starlight, Starman, Star of the Story, Star- ship, Stash, Stax,
Steam, Steamer, Steel, Stellar, Steph, Steve-O, Stevie, Sticky, Sting,
Stinger, Sting Ray, Stiletto,
Stinker, Stinky, Stitches, Stomper, Stone, Stone Cold, Stone
Man, Stoner, Stonewall, Stony, Storm, Storman, Storm
Front, Story, Story Teller, Straight, S-Train, Straw, Strawberry,
Strawberry Dream, Strawberry Shortcake, Straw

Man, Streaker, Street, Street Hustler, Street Wise, Stretch, Strictly Business, Strider, Strike, Striker, Stripes, Stroker, Strong, Strongman, Stub, Stubble, Stubble Head, Stubbs,

Stubby, Stud, Stumpy, Styles, Sub, Sub Man, Sub Zero,

Suede, Sug, Sugams, Sugar Babe, Sugar, Sugar Belly, Sugar Cake, Sugar Cookies, Sugar Dumplin, Sugar Free, Sugar Hill, Sugar Lips, Sugar and Spice, Sugar Plum, Sugar Ray,

Sultan, Summer, Sunshine, Sunshine Kiss, Superman, Super Smooth, Superstar, Supremacy, Supreme, Surprise, Surfer, Sure Thing, Surgeon, Survivor, Susie, Suzy,

Suzy Q, Swag, Swaggy, Swaggy P, Swede, Sweet, Sweet Cakes, Sweet Cheeks, Sweet Daddy, Sweet Dream, Sweetheart, Sweetie, Sweet Lou, Sweet Mama, Sweet-n-Sour, Sweet Thing, Sweetness, Sweet Obsession, Sweet Pea, Sweet Potato, Sweet Prince, Sweet Revenge, Sweet Sensation, Sweet Tea, Sweet Tater, Sweet Treat,

Sweets, Sweetums, Sweetwater, Swirl, Swish, Swiss, Sydney, Symbol, Syv

This is a cute nickname when you are a little. Not so sure as you get older.—Sleepy Head

I am not sure if your idol is Tony Montana or Al Capone with this nickname—Scarface

I am not sure what is positive about this nickname. Either your are not very cool or someone is describing your head.—Square

# T

# Nicknames that start with the Letter

## "T"

Tab, Tabasco, Tabby, Tadpole, Taffy, TaffyTag, Tahitian
Treat, Taj, Tang, Tangie, Tangerine, Tango, Tangy, Tank,
Tao, Tappy, Tarco, Tart, Tash, Tasha, Tasmanian, Tater, Tater Skins,
Tater Tot, Taxi Guy, Tay, Taylor Made, Tay-Tay, Taz, Tazman, Tot,
T-Bell, T-Bird, T-Bone, T-Boy, T-Boz, TC, TD, Tea, Tea Cup, Tea
Time, Tears, Tebo, Technical,
Technician, Teddy, Teddy Bear, Teddy Boo, Teddy Boy, Tee
Baby, Tee Tee, Tee Tot, Teezo, Telescope, Tennessee, Teo,
Terminator, Terminology. Terrible, Terror, Tex, Texas,
Theo, Thibbs, Thing, Thor, Thorax, Thorn, Thrilla,
Thumbelina, Thumbkin, Thump, Thumpy, Thumper, Thunder, Thunder
Bolt, Thunder Heart, Thunder Lips, Thunderstorm, Tia, Tico, Tic Tac,
Tic Toc, Tiff, Tiffy, Tig, Tiger, Tigger, Tiggy, Tigress, Till, Timber,
Timberland, Timekeeper
Timmy, Tin Man, Tink, Tinker Bell, Tinky, Tiny, Tip, Tippy,
Tipsy, Tito, Titus, Tizzle, TJ, TK, TMac, T-Neck, TNT,
Toad, Toast, Toasty, Toby, Toffee, Tomahawk, Tomb Boy,
Tom Cat, Tom Tom, Tone, Tonka, Tonsil, Tonza, Toodle
Bear, Toodles, Tooney, Tookie, Tootie, Tootie Fruity, Tooth
Pick, Tooter, Tootsie, Tootsie Bear, Tootsie Roll, Tootsie Wootsie,
Torch, Tornado, Toxic, Top Cat, Top Dog, Top
Gun, Top Hat, Toy, TP, Trace, Tractor, Tragedy, Tragic, Trail
Blazer, Train, Transformer, Trav, Tre, Treach, Trea Trea, Tree, Tree
Man, Tree Top, Tot, Trell, T, R., T-Rex, Trick,
Tricky, Trina, Trinity, Trio, Trip, Triple Threat, Triton, Trojan, Trompas,
Tron, Tronda, Trooper, Trout, Truck, Truff,

Truffle, Truffy, Tubby, Tuck, Tuff, Tuff Stuff, Tulip, Turbo, Turbo Man, Turk, Turnip, Turtle, Tush, Tushy Soft, Tutee Fruity, Tutone, Twain, Tweed, Tweedy, Tweety, Tweety-Bird, Twin, Twinkie, Twinkle, Twist, Twista, Twister, Two of A Kind, Two Legit, Two Ton, Ty, Tyga, Tyke, Typhoon, TV Guy, TV Man,

When I was growing up I had a fascination with dinosaurs.
The Jurassic park movies
have increased the
fascination of dinosaurs
for many. However I am
still not understanding
this nickname. Maybe this
person is the toughest of
the tough— T Rex

I guess you love that nice chewy
chocolaty taste or maybe you
just like the dance—Tootsie
Roll

This nickname usually describe someone's
body appearance or what they walk around
with in their mouth.—Toothpick

# Nicknames that start with the Letter "U"

Ultimate, Ultimate Male, Ultimate Warrior, Ump, Undeniable, Underdog, Unforgettable, Unguarded, Underestimated,

UG, Unicorn, Unique, Uniqueness, United, United Front, Unity, Universal, Universal Heartthrob, Unk, Unkle L, U know Me, Unnerved, Uno, Unpredictable, Unstoppable, Unstoppable Force, Untamed, Unthinkable, Uptown, Upward Bound, Upward Mobility, Urban Cowboy, Urban Legend,

US, Usher, Utopia

Yes this is our mother's or father's brother. Most times you are able to get quit a bit of money from him—Unk

Not much to say about this nickname. If it is your nickname then all I can ask is why? -
U
n
i
c
o
r
n

Normally this nickname signifies a particular sports occupation that one has.
—Ump

# Nick Names that start with the Letter "V"

Val, Valentino, Van, Vanilla, Vanilla Ice, Vanilla Red, Vanilla Smooth, Vanity, Vee, Vee Jay, Vega, Vegas, Vegas Jack, Vegas Von, Velcro, Veijo, Velvet, Velvet Rose, Touch, Vengeance, Vengeance Pimpin, Venture, Venus, Versace, Vertical,

Vet, Vett, Vic, Vice, Viceroy, Vidal, View Finder, Viewing Me, Vigorous One, Viking, Vikki, Villon, Vin, Vin Rock,

Vince, Victory, Vinnie, Vintage, Violent Storm, Violet, Violet Rose, Viper, Virus, Visionary, Vito, Viv, Vivi, Vixen,

Vogue, Volatile, Voltage, Von, Voo, Voyager Vulture

Either you are true representative of the great state of
Minnesota and its football team, or you truly are a man
of the ancient seas—
Viking

Unless this is short for your love for a nice cold treat,
if not then there can only be one prolific person
with this nickname in a life time—Vanilla Ice

One of the staples of our society is that
we all support our soldiers. If this is
your nickname based upon your great
service to our county then here is a
salute to you—Vet

# Nicknames that start with the Letter "W"

Wacko, Waddles, Waffle Dog, Waffle Ears, Waffler, Waldo,
Walk, Walkman, Walker, Walking by Faith, Wally, Walnut,
Wanting Nothing, War Eagle, Warrior, Watchman, Water Lilly, Water
Sprout, Wavy, Waxie, Waxman, WC, Weave,
Weed, Weeping, Wes, West, Wheat, Wheels, Wheezy,
Whirlpool Wiz, Whip, Whip Appeal, Whiskers, Whispers,
White Chocolate, White Flash, White Lightning, White Out,
Whitey, Who Dat, Wifey, Wiggle, Wiggles, Wiggle Worm, Wildcat,
Wild Child, Wildfire, Widdle Waddle, Wild Man, Wildside, Wild
Thang, Wild Thing, Wild and Witty, Wild
Woman, Wilky, Will, Willow, Willow Wonderer, Willy,
Wimpy, Wincy, Wind Jammer, Wind Jumper, Wind Maker, Wind
Rider, Wind Runner, Windago, Windy, Winky, Winky
Dinky, Winner, Winnie, Wit, Wisher, Wishful Thinking,
Wising on a Star, Wish Maker, Wiz, Wiz Kid, Wizard, Wizzle, Wobble,
Wobbler, Wolf, Wolfing, Wolf Man, Wolfy, Wolverine, Woman,
Wombing, Won Ton, Wood, Woody,
Woogie, Wookie, Wookie Bear, Wonder, Wonderer, Wonder
Boy, Wonderful, Wonderful Thing, Wop, World Class,
Worm, Worshiper, Worthwhile, Wrangler, Wrangling Man,
Wrecker, Wrigley, Wu, Wuz Good, Wuzzy

Someone with this nickname usually is someone who has some distinct knowledge or someone who has magical powers? - Wizard

I hope this nickname is really not because of your ears—Waffle Ears

This is one of those nicknames that is either describing you facial features or you are just fascinated with an old school disc jockey—Wolf man

# Nicknames that start with the Letter

# "X"

X
X-ample
X-Centric
X-Cite X-Con X-Dog
X-Exhibit xlon
X-Man X-Mate
XO
Xpadre X-Rated
X-Ray
X-Stinguisher
Xtra
Xtreme
XV

With this nickname you
are either a very
transparent person or you
can see through others
- X-Ray


This is one I
scratch my head
on but I guess it
can give you street
credits or it can be
a cool rap
name—X-Con

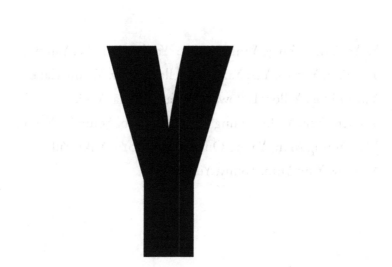

# Nicknames that start with the Letter "Y

Ya Ya, Yana, Yancy, Yank, Yankee, Yankee Doodle, Yanky, Yawning, Yay Yo, Yaz, Yazman, Yella, Yellow, Yellow Cake, Yellow Dog. Yellow Fellow, Ying-Yang, Yoda, Yogi, Yonker, York, Yorky, Young G, Young Gun, Youngin, Young MC, Young Man, Young One, Youser, YoYo, Yuki, Yukon, Yummy, Yum Yum, Yonny, Yurtle,

This nick name may be inspired by a toy that most of us over the age of 35 played with or you like the music of that prolific female rapper of the 90s—Yo-Yo

If you feel you are moist, sweet, buttery and creamy then this nickname makes sense for you—Yellow Cake

Either you are a good ole northern person or you love that dominate baseball team out of the sates of NEW YORK—Yankee

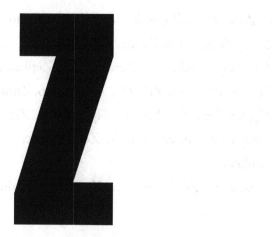

# Nicknames that start with the Letter

# "Z"

Z, Zace, Zach, Zand, Zandie, Zandit, Zandria, Zan, Zani,
Zane, Zany, Zave, Zavier, Zavy, Zay, Zay Zay, Zeb, Zebra, Zed, Zee
Zee, Zeke, Zelda, Zen, Zenith, Zero, Zepher, Zest Zesta, Zester, Zesty,
Zeta, Zetty, Zeus, Zia, Zib, Zibby, Zico, Zimbo, Zinc, Zig Zag, Ziggy,
Ziggler, Zip, Zip Appeal, Zip Me Up, Zipit, Zippin, Zippo, Zippy,
Zippy Kay, Zipster, Ziva, Zo, Zod, Zodiac, Zole, Zollie, Zombie, Zona,
Zonkers,
Zora, Zoro, Zory, Z-ro, Zsa Zsa, Zubie, Zulu

I know it is the big
thing right now but
I am just not sure
why you would want
to have this nick-
name—Zombie

If you have this nickname, I hope you
are as fresh as the soap—Zest

With this nick name, you better be good with a sword, At least
in your recreational time—Zoro

So here is what N thru Z looks like:

**Letter N (92)**

**Letter O (72) Letter P (195)**

**Letter Q (41) Letter R (161)**

**Letter S (404) Letter T (216)**

**Letter U (36) Letter V (60)**

**Letter W (112)**

**Letter X (18) Letter Y (36)**

**Letter Z (66)**

Cookies, Bears, Sugar, Rappers. and Cartoon Characters all make up some of the interesting nicknames in the second half of our list. Z to N nicknames consist of 1,509 different nicknames with the letters S (404) making up almost 27% of the total.

So there you have a list of about 3500+ common and unique nicknames from A to Z. Did your unique nickname make the list? Over the years I have had several nicknames and I close with those for your enjoyment:

**RodDog**

**Darren**

**Pin Cushion**

**Ra**

**Mr. B**

**Dee**

**B**

**#6**

**Big Rod**

## Your Assistance

If you have a unique and interesting nickname or if you know of someone with a unique and interesting nickname please send it in to us at bbv2mllc@gmail.com as we will be looking to get started on a volume 2 for your pleasure.

# Letter Nickname Index
## (Total Nicknames by Letter)

**Letter A (113)**

**Letter B (307)**

**Letter C (301)**

**Letter D (211)**

**Letter E (78)**

**Letter F (150)**

**Letter G (152)**

**Letter H (128)**

**Letter I (64)**

**Letter J (112)**

**Letter K (101)**

**Letter L (161)**

**Letter M (201)**

**Letter N (92)**

**Letter O (72)**

**Letter P (195)**

**Letter Q (41)**

**Letter R (161)**

**Letter S (404)**

**Letter T (216)**

**Letter U (36)**

**Letter V (60)**

**Letter W (112)**

**Letter X (18)**

**Letter Y (36)**

**Letter Z (66)**

# About the Author

Rodney Brooks is the president and founder of Brothers Brooks Vision 2 Mission LLC, and their mission is "To be the best in helping all people excel in all aspects in life." As a certified professional in human resource, Brooks meets many different people in his profession. One of the key elements is a person name or what they would like to be called—i.e., nickname. Having been given several different nickname in his own right Brooks decided to embark on how many different and unique nicknames he could come up with. Living in the south, he is well aware that the nickname is just as important as the real name. It does not matter if you live in Little Rock, Arkansas; Atlanta, Georgia; Memphis, Tennessee; or his current resident of Meridian, Mississippi. Having given his four children some unique names, it seemed only fitting for him to have a little fun and see all the interesting nicknames that are out there.